AF484677

When the Streetlights Come On

—A Memoir—

Written and illustrated by

J. FRANK WYNNE

Silent Night
PUBLISHING

Thanks to my boys (men)
Kevin Doyle and Paul Staub for confirming that this effort was worth
pursuing and surprising me by offering to help write.
Mark Zemil, for being an honest sounding board throughout this
endeavor and for contributing to the Foreword.
Jim Poulos for his Foreword description of young J. Frank.
Vincent Wynne and his illustration critiques

An Extra special thanks to all the girls (ladies)!
My friend and colleague Felicity Fox for lighting up when we first discussed
the book and her continued enthusiasm and review of the first draft.
Marti Spaulding for her smile and laughter while assisting with research.
Editors Michele McEvoy, Allison Marea, and Kim Baer
for their skills and kind encouragement.
Hannah Wynne for her editorial tough love and web design.
Andy Haas Schneider, book design, a Godsend and Baby Boomer.
Cara Swartwout and Karen Rashmir for their unwavering support.
Alena Hart, energy grid expert and utility pole visual consultant.
Nora Jones' music accompanied me during my many days of painting
illustrations. Her music fit the creative experience beautifully.
Soobie! My ever-supportive wife. She stood beside me on this
adventure and so many more. Soobie always gives me straight talk
without the sugar coating. She told me if something was just plain bad,
and as well as when I got it right.

Silent Night
PUBLISHING

jfrankwynne.com

ISBN: 979-8-218-95308-9

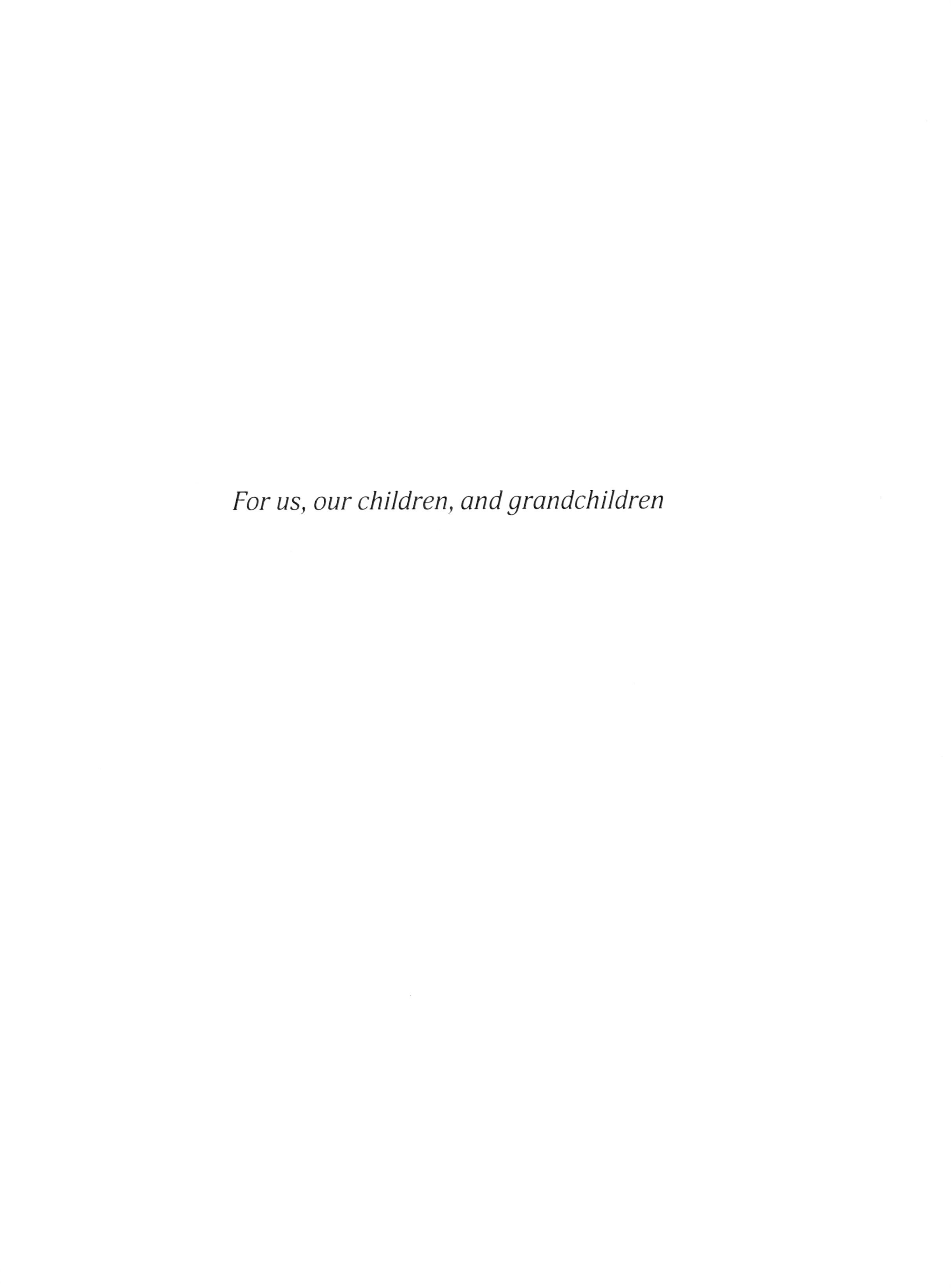

For us, our children, and grandchildren

foreword

13-year-old J. Frank Wynne

I met Frank when I was in the fourth grade through a mutual friend who was a neighbor of his. We hit it off right away. Frank was thoughtful and deep thinking; even-tempered but would mix-it-up if needed. We all loved to play rough sports like tackle football and our neighborhood variation "Maul-ball." I'm sure many other neighborhoods had similar names for it. Frank and I were the only ones of our peers who loved to play strategic board games— usually, World War II or the Civil War. We would play for hours. Around age 13, girls were becoming a big distraction. We both belonged to the community pool which was always a goldmine for our newest pursuits. We did seem to laugh a lot. Between the different families and all the characters in the neighborhood I'm surprised we still aren't laughing.

— K.D.

Clever, artistic, and keenly observant, nothing escaped his notice. From a caricature, well-timed quip, or a parody of a current TV show or movie classic, Frank had the ability to embarrass, captivate, and make a room full of classmates double over in pain to keep from laughing during any classroom exercise.

— J.P.

I remember him as a very inquisitive young man who would push the boundaries yet never actually step over the lines. With the woods and a creek just steps away from his house, there was always plenty of room for exploring, building forts, and making up our own fun and games.

— M.Z.

While reflecting on the old neighborhood with my childhood friend Kevin, he enthusiastically added, "We didn't have anything and didn't expect anything. We would go outside and find things to do. I wouldn't trade those times for anything." Those were exactly my feelings too. I wondered if maybe more of our generation feel the same way. After many interviews and conversations with old friends, yes, they do!

Somewhere between little kid and early teenager, from 1967 to 1972, the days slowed, seeming significantly longer than in later adult years. Children gathered socially to play outdoors. We had not heard the term Baby Boomers but that is who we are. Our outdoor world helped us develop social coping skills apart from direct parental supervision. I learned about group interaction and how natural pecking orders evolve.

I lived in the present; time practically stood still. I shared an improvising spirit, played sports in our neighborhood fields, and exploited the seasonal opportunities of changing weather. I was great at playing—it was what I did best!

Our parents endured the great depression, served in WWII and the Korean War, and were central pillars of middle America. The Vietnam conflict was ongoing, but our modest world was safe. The best place for kids was outdoors and out from under foot. "Go outside and play," was the usual order of the day. So, after taking out the trash, cleaning my room, finishing homework (or maybe not), I ran out the door, down the steps, and up the street to see who and what I would find.

These vignettes and illustrations portray the energetic lightheartedness of carefree days I recall with great fondness. The illustrations show moments of action that kept us laughing and our hearts racing in the throes of pure fun.

The ending of the black-and-white 1941 movie *Citizen Kane*, says it so well. Replace "Rosebud" with "Flexible Flyer," and transport to the pure irreplaceable fun and freedom of the late 1960s and early 1970s.

Our house was not air conditioned when I was growing up. During milder weather we slept with the windows open. Any attempts to sleep in late were often interrupted by the drone of a power mower, children's voices, screams and laughter, or the rhythmic thud of footsteps running across the yards.

It was always great to have visitors. Sometimes mom would call up the stairs, "Mark is here to see you!" "Jeez, I'm not ready, better get moving." Moments later, the cocky red head would bound up the stairs to my second-story bedroom to see what was going on. He was interchangeable with any number of the assorted characters who stopped by. In no time I'd get ready, tie my sneakers, and run as quickly out of the house as possible. The idea was to get out of earshot so Mom wouldn't freeze me in place and reel me back in to complete unfinished chores.

On days when Mom announced, "Get dressed and go outside," I never argued. Once outside, the day would unwind in a series of engaging activities. My adventures began. If no one was around, I would knock on a neighbor's door to go inside, or he would come out. That's how I grew to know entire families – parents, grandparents, aunts, uncles, brothers, sisters, and cousins.

"Holy cow, did you see that?" was a question I always wanted to answer, "yes." Events with low probability, like the amazing bounce of a ball, an equally incredible catch, or a bicycle wreck where the rider emerged unscathed, had to be seen firsthand. If I couldn't answer with something like, "Yeah, that was unbelievable!" then to those who did see, it meant I had totally missed it. I couldn't replay or rewind, so it paid to always be alert. To see was to believe.

The only outdoor rule...

"Be home when the streetlights come on."

10

football

We had our sandlot version of football. In our league, everyone was eligible to play the entire game. You didn't need to make the team or earn the coach's favor. Players were divided evenly by skill or age to make for better competition.

I would walk up to the top of the street and start kicking or passing the football with another kid, anticipating that others would be lured outside. Soon, players for three-on-three or four-on-four teams would appear and pair off.

When playing quarterback, I diagrammed plays in the dirt using a twig, drew with my index finger on the chest of the kid playing center, or drew invisibly on the palm of my hand. These were not ordinary diagrams; every play was designed to score a touchdown. Elements of speed, surprise, and exploitation of opponents' weaknesses were factored into every play.

Thankfully, no parents ever oversaw our games. We debated foul plays and settled penalties ourselves. Sometimes a call was disputed for the sake of just winning the argument. If you wrongly disputed a foul, you were a jerk. You knew it, and your friends knew it too. If we were tired and irritable it was best to call the game before confrontations escalated. Fair play generally prevailed.

If there were not enough players for two teams, we would play Maul the Man with the Ball, or Maul-ball for short. It worked like this: Throw the football to one man and the rest of us would tackle him. Once down on the ground, the runner had to release the ball. Some hesitancy to pick up the ball was normal while surrounded by guys waiting to pounce. The football had to be picked up fast, or the man with the ball got hit and went down hard.

Until it was outlawed, the seventh and eighth-grade boys played Maul-ball on the school asphalt parking lot that doubled as a playground. One evening, while playing a hybrid combination of Maul-ball and King of the Hill, Kevin and I partially detached Al's ear by tackling him by his head and pulling him in opposite directions. We were extra nervous when he ran home. I didn't get in trouble though. His dad used black electrical tape to reattach his ear to his head, and all was well.

> *. . . I diagrammed plays in the dirt using a twig, drew with my index finger on the chest of the kid playing center, or drew invisibly on the palm of my hand.*

We played in any type of weather; overcast was preferred to sunny. Throw your good buddy to the ground for a mud slide or fling him across the wet grass—unpredictability made the rough-housing more entertaining. I was never disciplined for getting filthy, but when dirt was tracked into the house or my clothes did not end up in the basement by the washing machine, I knew that I would hear about it.

MONOPOLY
MONOPOLY

Christmas

My mother was totally into Christmas. Shopping for the perfect Christmas tree at the Saint John's Boy Scout tree stand would take forever. She took as long at picking out a tree as she did shopping for lingerie. Pick up a tree, unravel the twine, hold it up, put it back, inspect another… It tested my patience to have trees I thought were fine rejected one after another. Ultimately, Mom would be proud of her decorated tree.

Mom's Christmas Eve gathering tradition continued for more than 45 years. Her evening fare included homemade fudge, honey ham, tangerines, and hard candies. At the end of the evening, I would walk up the hill to the Old Church and face the challenge of making it through the entire midnight mass. I would wake up embarrassed when a kind adult tapped me on their way out of church. I staggered back home to find the immediate family opening a few gifts. After all, it was after midnight and technically Christmas Day!

A board game was practically guaranteed to show up under the tree. If a box landed under the tree before the big day, I tested my psychic abilities to determine the contents. I could never resist and had to shake the present, so similar in shape to a clothes box. The rattling sounds within were a dead give-away. Nothing compares to the smell of a new Milton Bradley or Parker Brothers board game box being torn from its cellophane wrapper. The dice and game pieces were slippery and new. I observed how others played the games and gained insights into their personalities. How they played the games revealed good sports, poor losers, gloating winners, cheaters, and negotiators. Older players took losing as a major affront to their big-kid status, one even tipped the game board over to avoid a loss. I could never beat a particular friend at Monopoly – an unforgettable, humiliating statistic.

A board game was practically guaranteed to show up under the tree. If a box landed under the tree before the big day, I tested my psychic abilities to determine the contents.

Some of my favorite games of the day are still around.

Stratego

Sorry

MONOPOLY

Trouble

Clue

The Game of LIFE

Yahtzee

RISK

Chess

After the gifts were opened and the post-present elation waned, I would be back outside or over to friends' houses to check out their gifts.

CAR

sledding

My cousin recently greeted me at a family gathering, "We use to play…!" she recalled enthusiastically. She was partly referring to a stay with my family during winter school break. That December brought enough snow to sleigh ride from the top of Church-hill all the way to the bottom of our street, a good 150-yard glide. We've shared those quality-time recollections and interactions our entire lives. We love each other and those memories, and our bond has always remained strong.

Hand-me-down black rubber boots that fit over my shoes with thin metal clips to fasten closed were standard issue in the early 60s. I'm not sure where the hand-me-down boots came from, but my mom clipped me into them for the first time when I was very small. I was hot and resembled the Michelin Man by the time Mom let me out the front door. After a few winters of use and storage in the basement, the clips would break to the point of having only one or two left to close the boot.

Snow spilled down the front of those black boots and socks would slide halfway off in my shoes. My thin woolen mittens or gloves would have clumps of snow that adhered like Velcro and wouldn't come off until it melted. We peeled off the snowy layers just inside the front door of our house. If the boots fit tightly (before I inherited my brother's larger size), they would end up pulling off my shoes and leaving them stuck inside the boot. Snow-play later improved with the new insulated hard rubber boots that were worn directly over socks. The insulated boots, which sold in a more stylish green or brown color, lengthened the outdoor snow time, keeping my feet warm and dry longer. The quality of the gloves also improved. No matter how I was equipped, it was a must to venture into every snowstorm.

My wood and metal Flexible Flyer sled laid in the yard all year long. Come winter, the rusted metal runners would stop dead, even on ice. I dragged my sled across asphalt or concrete rough enough for abrasive rust removal. Then I would go into the basement to find a piece of my dad's sandpaper. After fine sanding, I rubbed bar soap across the runners for maximum slide – ready to go! For just one to three days and evenings a year, the sledding was superb while the snow conditions held up. I just had to sled until exhausted, half frozen, or injured.

It was commonplace for a group of us to go sledding at night. The crisp winter air was clean and quiet, the only sound was the snow crunching under foot. The sledding course was either down the hill and straight into the street, or down the other hill and across the street. Drivers were always careful and looked out for us; they were used to having kids fly out from any direction. We watched out for the cars as well as for each other. Overall, until the snow either deteriorated from sand-truck road applications or melted, we would sled after school and again after dinner. A day or two later, when the snow was reduced to a few small, wet, and compactable piles, snowball fights ensued. A head shot always incited enthusiastic laughter and immediate whimpers.

I hit an adult neighbor in the chest with a snowball after he warned me not to. He started after me, chasing me through the back yards and onto the next street. Halfway around the block he was still coming for me. Running as fast as possible through the drifts and compacted street snow, I stayed ahead of him on the turn back down from the top of my street. I knew he was gaining ground. I ran fast, thinking I couldn't let him catch me on the final 50-yard sprint to my house. At just the right moment my neighbor Reed opened his front door and yelled for me to take refuge inside.

J. Frank Wynne

baseball

From the time the snow nearly melted in late February, until the grassy fields grew too tall in May, we were playing baseball. We played 500, where the batter hit the ball out of his own hand and the fielders' scored points. A fly catch in the air was worth 100 points. One bounce scored 75, two bounces 50, and a grounder 25. Once a fielder scored 500 points, he became the batter. 500 turned into ball games after a round or two.

After the preseason warm-ups, real games began. We piled up leaves or twigs for the bases. The fields were lumpy with potholes. The pitcher lobbed the ball across the parking lot driveway of the Knights of Columbus, and the side of the building served as the backstop. A hard-hit ball wasn't predictable and would go in any direction on the first hop. I decided early on to eliminate the risk of the odd bounce. I was fast and could run down a fly ball, so I played outfield. A great hit knocked the ball out of the field, down the short embankment, and into Old Man Chambers' front yard. Full of fear and adrenaline, I had to run and get the ball before Chambers came out his front door. He never said anything to us, but always came off his front porch and motioned like he intended to confiscate the ball.

There were thousands of gnats everywhere in early Spring. I remember the smell of the leather glove held in front of my face as a bug shield, peering out between the web and palm of the glove while waiting for the next hit. Gnats would get in my eyes and my inner ears, buzzing around in my head. When I got home I would fill a shot glass with water, tilt my head, and hold it against my ear to flush out the gnats.

When the games shifted over to the elementary school field, we would hit the ball out of the park and into the adjoining woods. Although that was a great hit, it could delay or end the game since we only had one hardball among us. I'd have to kick around in the crispy leaves until the lost ball was uncovered. We used baseballs until they were knocked apart. The yarn streamed behind the core like a kite tail once the leather cover detached.

We played catch in the street if there were only two of us. When a throw was missed, the ball would shoot down the street, bounce off the curb just missing the sewer opening, or go straight into the storm drain. A good thundershower would wash the baseball down the hill to where the street dead-ended at the woods. Somewhere in the drainage ditch, we found our lost brown baseballs.

A nickel bought five baseball cards and a flat, stale, rectangular piece of bubble gum. The gum gave the cards a flavorful, new, edible smell. I had Roberto Clemente, Willie Mays, Roger Marris, Jim Wynn, and a stack of others in my collection. Students would flip cards at school by tossing them frisbee-like against the brick wall of the school. Our asphalt playground went all the way up to the building. Whose ever card was closest to the wall won the opponents' card. A "leaner" against the wall was unbeatable. In third grade I played against an eighth grader, and one time was enough to know better. Losing cards to him at that incredible rate was unsustainable. Years later, all of my baseball cards disappeared shortly after I moved out. Many Baby Boomers suffered the same disappearing collection fate.

Late in the season, lazy sunsets lengthened the sweet summer evenings. Daylight faded while my eyes continued to adjust. When the baseball was no longer visible, it was reason to call the game. The slightly sweaty sheen on heads and torsos began to evaporate in the cooling evening air. Distinct evening sounds signaled it was finally time to go inside.

biking

I rode my bike on the streets throughout the neighborhood. The roads were marked with the burnt rubber of a Z-28 and other big block muscle cars whose noise gave us fair warning to move out of the way well in advance.

One bike was all I got, and it lasted a long time. I received my first and only one on Christmas day 1967 when I was 10. It was dark red, had monkey handlebars, and a banana seat. I attached baseball cards to the forks with clothespins to give the bike a cool flipp'n engine sound when the cards hit the spokes.

Walking or riding our bikes was the primary mode of transportation for visiting friends. The world was much bigger when we walked and became a bit smaller as we biked. The biking domain was about one square mile. While my father was at work, the only family vehicle was unavailable for taxiing. Even when Dad was home, I rarely bothered him for a ride. A bike gave me the freedom to travel to other neighborhoods.

Rubber handlebar grips would wear thin and fall off from too many side drops. On some winter evenings I stayed out too long and had to hold on to grip-less chrome monkey handlebars with numb bare hands. On one ride, I was far from home in the chilly dusk knowing I had to make it back despite the cold. Everyone else was in for dinner and there was no way to phone home to ask for a ride. I should have listened to Mom and worn gloves. Mom would say, "Run your hands under cold water." Warm water burned small fingers bordering on frost bite.

The bikes were sturdy, built well. Mine was left out on the side of the house all year long, covered by the snow, soaked by the rain, and baked by the sun. A bike could only get so rusty if it was ridden frequently enough. A little bit of oil on the chain, pumped-up tires, and straightened handlebars constituted a tune up.

One bike was all I got, and it lasted a long time. I received my first and only one on Christmas day 1967 when I was 10. It was dark red, had monkey handlebars, and a banana seat.

Leash laws did not yet exist. Dogs roamed free. Dog-doo was everywhere. Usually, the dogs were not a problem. One exception was an angry mutt that charged me, growling and barking as I started on a downhill street. His ambush gave me an adrenaline jolt. I un-straddled the seat and stood left foot on the left pedal. I coasted and gained speed while the dog ran, barked, and snapped viciously on the right. Gradually he lost the chase as the bike rolled faster. When out and traveling about, we did our best to solve our own problems.

outdoors

My neighborhood seemed huge and I explored every square foot of it. A few notable landmarks were the hollow tree, frog rock, church hill, and the historic graveyard. Air was cleaner and lawns were full of clover, dandelions, and buttercups, all of which attracted honeybees. Homeowners had not started to use weed killer or lawn applications. The Springtime combination of plants carpeting the lawns made for a honeyed green and yellow flavor. We would run barefoot across the yards. There were so many honeybees that I just had to aggravate them. Yes, I got stung a few times.

At the age of 12, my foot was finally large enough for the smallest, size 3, Chuck Taylor tennis shoe. My allotment was one pair a year. Black or white, high top or low, those were the choices. The greasers would wear the high-top black ones and "skunk" the back seam with Clorox bleach. By the end of the year the diamond pattern on the sole was worn smooth except for the holes in ball of the foot or heel where the foam rubber under-sole would soak up water on wet days. That's when the shoes stunk after staying damp for too long.

I built forts in my back yard, and in the woods. Supplies were sparse. Straightening bent nails to fasten boards without splitting the dry old wood were my first carpentry lessons.

In the Springtime, we scoured the woods for discarded parts to build go-cart coasters. For my first prototype I nailed 3 eight-penny nails through the center of each wheel hole and into the 2 x 4 frame. It wouldn't roll at all. Good axles were hard to find and crucial for a smooth ride. We pushed the go-carts up to the top of Church hill and rode them down and around the turn to the bottom of the street.

To me, the woods almost always smelled good. Sweet in May, earthy in Fall, and green in Summer. A creek flowed from the end of the neighborhood street all the way through to Rock Creek Park and into the Potomac River. In Summer, it was always much cooler by the creek no matter how hot and humid the weather. Crayfish, box turtles, and tadpoles were great finds.

Without a watch I could closely tell time by the position of the sun in the sky. In the afternoon, school let out at 3:00, a half mile away the 4:00 PM train whistle blew. Traffic would begin to get heavier at 5:00. I knew the afternoon was getting late and the evening beginning, when the church bells rang the Angelus a 6:00. On Sunday morning, the bell in the old church tower would ring at 9:50 AM to give get-out-of-bed notice that mass would begin in 10 minutes.

An empty non-recyclable glass bottle thrown out of a car window had a trade-in value of five cents. I started off on the half mile walk to Fowler's Market with my sister, brother, or neighbor. We knew we would find enough discarded bottles along the way to buy penny candies and maybe a soda. Without weekly allowances, we were pickers of sorts. Fowler stocked Nehi, Royal Crown Cola, Orange Crush, Fanta, and Coke. I remember the Dr. Pepper bottle had a silk-screened painted label. Fireballs, Bit O' Honey, and Mary Janes were some of my favorite penny candies. Lik-m-aid, Necco Wafers, and Good and Plenty cost five cents. The walk back home was uphill and was always longer than the walk to the market.

We played in the street a lot. We played catch and rode homemade coasters and bicycles. Everything was more durable. Over-engineered automobile bodies never dented when hit with a punted football, missed baseball, or a mischievous snowball. Thank goodness because repair costs never even occurred to me.

Soda and beer cans were thicker then, and no one recycled. They were discarded, available, and tough. I had a great arm and scored enough rock hits to sink them in the creek. Our throwing arms rarely got tired.

I shared a sense of freedom, responsibility, and self-governance with the other kids.

the pool

The neighborhood pool was the summer hangout….

All summer long, from the Memorial Day sunburn to the last day of Labor Day Weekend, I walked through the shaded woods and step-stoned across the creek to go swimming. I became ultra-efficient by wearing only my bathing suit to the pool, no towel, no shirt, and no shoes.

I swam until the lifeguard blew the whistle for adult swim, or even longer if I stayed in the water without the guards questioning my age. I could spend all day at the pool, surviving only on drinks from the water fountain if necessary. Fortunately, the Good Humor man would stop by twice a day. Ten cents would buy an ice cream sandwich, 25 cents would get you a Toasted Almond Bar.

I could sing the Frito Bandito song under water. My friend Patrick would request the song and we would both take a big breath and submerge at the deep end. I could see his eyes widen as my mouth closed, nasal version of the song began, "Ai Yi Yi Yi, I am the Frito Bandito." In one convulsive laugh he would release all the air from his lungs at once. Watching his face explode with an air bubble blast, underwater exhale eruption, made me do the same. Our heads popped out of the water, and we gasped and laughed simultaneously.

Tag, Marco Polo, chicken fights, and water wrestling were games we played. Splash fights and dunking had not yet been banned in public pools. The guards were a little older, so they got a little bit of auto-respect in our prisoner/guard relations. The lifeguard had us sit under the lifeguard stand as punishment for disobeying the rules, like no running on the deck. We protested the calls but had to serve our time. The girls liked the way the guards confidently strutted in their Speedo bathing suits. Sorry Gen X, it's our fault you guys couldn't breathe or blink without the lifeguard blowing the whistle at you.

Each summer there would be one pool party for the teens, which included a live band. I can remember listening to the neighborhood band play the songs of Cream and Three Dog Night from my front yard before I was old enough to attend.

Tag, Marco Polo, chicken fights, and water wrestling were games we played.

In late summer, the pool stayed open until 9:30 PM. Sometimes after the official closing, a water polo match was held across the deep end of the pool. The water stayed warmer than the evening air, so it was more pleasant for me to stay in the water than get out in the chilled air. Once out of the water, I would shiver-dry as fast as possible. The path home through the woods was familiar enough to walk the 100 yards in the pitch dark. I'd walk carefully in bare feet, senses on alert, listening for the boogeyman or most likely one of the neighbors.

I walked home, somewhat expended, smelling like chlorine, sporting pruney fingers and toes.

girls

Girls tended to be segregated from the boys up until the age of 13 or 14 . . . was it intentional? Us boys were not quite sure what they did evenings and weekends. They were exceptional at jumping one or two ropes at a time. The great ones were first-round picks for kickball games. Girls matured faster and were sometimes stronger and taller than the boys in fifth and sixth grades.

We made the first skateboards by nailing the wheels of girls' roller skates to 2 x 4s. Roller skates were fastened in the center by a wingnut and bolt, they came apart easily into two halves. Skates were designed to loosen so the size could be adjusted.

If I was anything like my son and his friends, I was a smelly little stinker and that was reason enough for the girls to stay away.

Additionally, I wore a veneer of second-hand smoke, compliments of my indoor chain-smoking parents.

Parochial school was a fancy name for Catholic school. The boys were always separated from the girls. It perpetuated a boys-against-the-girls culture.

In seventh grade, the girls in public school began to walk down my street in twos and threes. I would check them out from a distance and engage them in short, self-conscious conversations, sure that I would say the wrong thing and earn, "you're gross," or "I can't believe you said that." Interaction was awkward after the no-holds-barred banter with the guys in cut-down battles, where the best humorous insults won. The loser was humiliated by the observers' laughter. Most insulting names began with the letter "D" — dillweed, dufus, dork, and dweeb. Spazz was less offensive.

By eighth grade, kids were going steady and breaking up regularly.

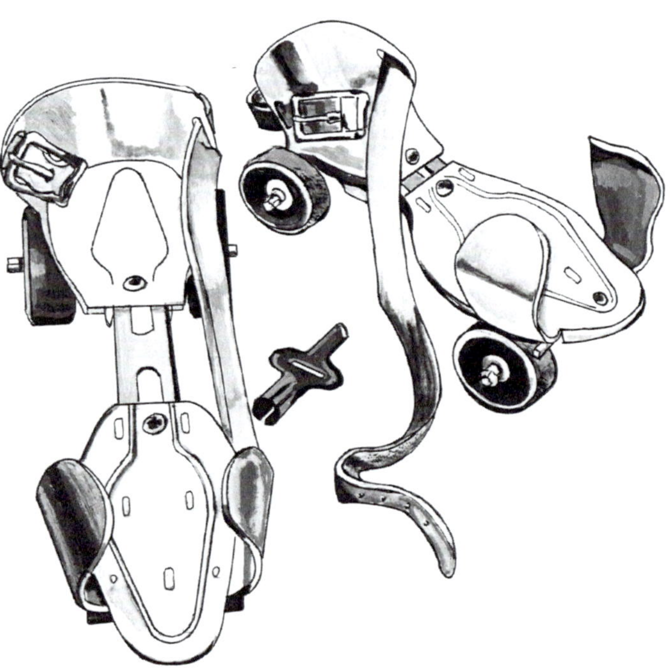

friends' memories

M.Z. – "Be sure to include a vignette that begins with your mother telling you to go outside and play because she wanted to clean the house. You were not allowed to get dirty. You had to enter the house from the side door then strip and take a shower, because you ALWAYS got dirty."

R.Z. – "We built a fort across the street in no man's land beyond the weeds."

M.Z. – "We went to the field and played sports like b-ball, and knocker, especially in the summer when the county recreation department operated an organized program. At night we played hide and seek and kickball."

S.W. – "We used to take roller skates and nail them to a two by four and make the first skateboards."

R.Z. – "Going down to the creek and walking, hopscotch, four-square, jump rope, dodgeball, sleeping in tents on our own property."

M.Z. – "Indoor games on rainy days- Rock'em Sock'em Robots, electric football, Skittleball, carroms."

A.G. – "I played football on my knees against the younger kids."

P.N. – "I could tell where the guys were gathering when a house had all their bikes in the front yard."

G.S. – "We played Barbies and set up tents in the back yard for sleepovers and played flashlight tag at night. We listened to 45s on the record player."

T.C. – "We rode our bikes everywhere and had to be home by evening."

J.T. – "Playing Red Rover in the Baltimore City back alley with the neighbor kids."

K.D. – "I floated plastic model ships in the creek and blew them up."

T.R. – "We played kick the can in the evening under the streetlight."

M.S. – "My brother and I rode our bikes through the alleys by our home in SE, DC. One day we stopped at a honey suckle vine and stayed until we sipped the nectar out of every flower on the vine."

A.S. – "We used to put bread bags over our shoes to help them slide into our boots and add a little more water proofing."

G.S. – "Red Rover, Red Rover . . ."

games we played

Football
Baseball
Hide and Seek
Lightning bug jars with airholes
Wrestling
Tag
Red Rover
Crack the Whip
Horseback riding
BB guns
Kick the Can
Tire Swings
Chinese Jump Rope
Hopscotch
Four Square
Play Army
Dodgeball
Fly kites
Acorn battles
Body surfing and sandcastles
HO Racetracks
Horseshoes

*If the day ended without a scrape, bad
bruise, or a pulled muscle, it was a good day!*

in closing

I didn't pay attention to the news or popular culture of the time. Events and trends just sort of happened around me while the significant stuff, like building a treehouse, finding a rope swing, or gathering and engaging my friends continued. Adolescence and early teen years were easy—we had grown into bigger and stronger versions of ourselves, and we were used to the program. We became game theorists. My curiosity was always heightened by the next discovery one of the other kids would make, like standing out in a field trying to attract bats with walkie-talkies as they emerged from the belfry at dusk. We laughed all the time. Seems to me we laughed for about five years straight. Nothing was perfect, and we knew that was the way it was.

Peer pressure, social influence, working, and making important choices would come along soon enough. When we started staying out past dark, some kids had rough goes of it in the years following. We helped each other, but teen support was not always enough. I salute my friends who made it through the turbulent years of young adulthood. If all of us had held true to our parents' guidance of "Don't do something just because everyone else is doing it," we would have been better focused on what mattered most.

My memories are dirty-boy pure. Interactions involved conscience and self-governance. I look back—and many Baby Boomers who inspired me do too—on the unrefined content of those days with incredible fondness.

Regularly, in every way, we exhausted ourselves. My legs often ached when I laid down for the night.